JAPANESE PROVERBS

WIT AND WISDOM

日本の
ことわざ

DAVID GALEF

illustrated by **JUN HASHIMOTO**

TUTTLE Publishing

Tokyo | Rutland, Vermont | Singapore

"Books to Span the East and West"

Tuttle Publishing was founded in 1832 in the small New England town of Rutland, Vermont [USA]. Our core values remain as strong today as they were then—to publish best-in-class books which bring people together one page at a time. In 1948, we established a publishing office in Japan—and Tuttle is now a leader in publishing English-language books about the arts, languages and cultures of Asia. The world has become a much smaller place today and Asia's economic and cultural influence has grown. Yet the need for meaningful dialogue and information about this diverse region has never been greater. Over the past seven decades, Tuttle has published thousands of books on subjects ranging from martial arts and paper crafts to language learning and literature—and our talented authors, illustrators, designers and photographers have won many prestigious awards. We welcome you to explore the wealth of information available on Asia at www.tuttlepublishing.com.

Published by Tuttle Publishing, an imprint of Periplus Editions (HK) Ltd.

www.tuttlepublishing.com

Copyright © 1987, 2000, 2012 by David Galef and Jun Hashimoto

Library of Congress Cataloging-in-Publication Data
Japanese proverbs : wit and wisdom / compiled and translated by David Galef ; illustrated by Jun Hashimoto.
224 p. : ill. ; 23 cm.
Japanese proverbs with English translations for the language learner.
Includes index.
ISBN 978-4-8053-1200-1 (pbk.)
1. Proverbs, Japanese--Translations into English. 2. Proverbs, Japanese. 3. Proverbs, English. 4. Japanese language--Conversation and phrase books--English. I. Galef, David. II. Hashimoto, Jun, ill.
PN6519.J3J356 2012
398.9'956--dc23
2011052444

ISBN 978-4-8053-1200-1

Distributed by

North America, Latin America & Europe
Tuttle Publishing
364 Innovation Drive
North Clarendon, VT 05759-9436 U.S.A.
Tel: 1 (802) 773-8930
Fax: 1 (802) 773-6993
info@tuttlepublishing.com
www.tuttlepublishing.com

Japan
Tuttle Publishing
Yaekari Building, 3rd Floor, 5-4-12 Osaki,
Shinagawa-ku, Tokyo 141 0032
Tel: (81) 3 5437-0171
Fax: (81) 3 5437-0755
sales@tuttle.co.jp
www.tuttle.co.jp

Asia Pacific
Berkeley Books Pte. Ltd.
3 Kallang Sector #04-01
Singapore 349278
Tel: (65) 6741-2178
Fax: (65) 6741-2179
inquiries@periplus.com.sg
www.tuttlepublishing.com

First edition
24 23 22 21   10 9 8 7   2104VP

Printed in Malaysia

Contents

Japanese Proverbs

Preface

It's hard to believe that twenty-five years have passed since the publication of our first Japanese proverbs book, *Even Monkeys Fall from Trees*. In 1987, the internet was still medium-sized, cell phones were a luxury, and I was still in graduate school. In life's slow shift from youthful enthusiasm to middle-aged experience, I was nearer the start. Collecting and translating Japanese proverbs was a labor of love, and it resulted in my first book. I certainly didn't expect to profit much from the endeavor.

Since its first publication, the book has gone into multiple printings. A companion volume, *Even a Stone Buddha Can Talk*, came out in 2000. Longevity is a testament to success or sometimes just inertia, but to be in print after so long still feels good. In 2011, Tuttle approached me about publishing a combined and annotated edition. By then, I had published a fair amount and knew that a book, any book, involves a great deal of time and effort. Still, how difficult could expansion and revision be?

Going back to my original work, I found that most of the material remains timely, or as timeless a proverb. On the other hand, some of the translations sounded awkward, and a few of the Western equivalents seemed off, or at least required amplification. This observation led to the addition of a short explanatory paragraph for each translation. The paragraphs provide anything from extra meaning to cultural context and occasionally another proverb for comparison's sake. The new apparatus makes the combined volume more of a useful reference work. But the playful illustrations remain, as well as the back-and-forth nature of the book, wherein one can start with a proverb and guess about its parallel on the other side of the globe.

In the process of revision, I altered a few proverb translations and Western equivalents. For the benefit of readers who want to know the original meanings, I've tried to stick close to the literal rather than translate loosely. I also debated whether to drop some entries that have proved over the years either too obscure for even most Japanese, or mere phrases rather than full-blown proverbs. *Yoki funbetsu wa setchin de deru,* "Wise judgment comes when on the toilet," is an example of the first problem, but I admire the underlying idea. *Suna o kamu,* "To chew sand," is an instance of the second issue, simply an expression, but I like the image. In the end, I decided to keep them all, but flag the few that might raise eyebrows on both sides of the Pacific. This is an informed volume.

The advertiser's phrase "New and improved!" may be a tired gambit, but it seems appropriate here. To quote a proverb added in one of the explanatory paragraphs: *Furuki o tazunete atarashiki o shiru*: "To understand new things, study the old." And scholarship need not be a solitary endeavor: once again, I gratefully acknowledge the assistance of Jun Hashimoto, Michiko Hashimoto, and Beth Weinhouse.

—David Galef, 2012

Foreword
Even Monkeys Fall from Trees

The primary definition of "proverb" in the *Oxford English Dictionary* is very careful: "A short pithy saying in common and recognized use; a concise sentence, often metaphorical or alliterative in form, which is held to express some truth ascertained by experience or observation and familiar to all; an adage, a wise saw."

The three words before "express" follow the advice of *Atama kakushite shiri kakusazu* (English equivalent: "Protect yourself at all points"): foresee challenges and attacks and take measure against them. If the Oxford did as the small desk dictionaries I have with me do, and dispensed with the qualification, then the definition would be in error. Sometimes proverbs fly in the face of "experience or observation," and sometimes a proverb will contradict another one. *Kyō no yume, Ōsaka no yume* (no. 50) is vague and subject to several interpretations, some not completely in accord with common sense. Several proverbs advising caution are contradicted by *Koketsu ni irazumba koji o ezu* (no. 88), urging us to trespass upon a tigress's den.

Proverbs are what people are always saying. In this they are akin to cliches, but they are different from cliches in that they have a touch of poetry. They make lively use of imagery and they are sensitive to the music of language. They say the things that people think important in ways that people remember. They express common concerns. So a collection of proverbs is a compact treatise on the values of culture. Matching sets of proverbs from two cultures make a treatise in comparative sociology, or cultural anthropology.

It need not surprise us, though it should interest us, that the same proverbs are to be found in very different cultures. The lot of the human race is similar the world over. That not all the proverbs of one culture are to be found in another need not surprise us either, and it should interest us very much. It demonstrates that the concerns of the two are not identical. It ought to shake us a little from our parochialism.

Inevitably, Mr. Galef does not always find perfect English matches for his Japanese proverbs. Some of his equivalents do not sound like proverbs, and some do not seem precisely equivalent. He makes note in his Preface of an excellent example, the one about the nail that sticks out (no. 43). "Don't make waves" is ingenious, but it seems more an injunction to moderation than to conformity. The heart of the matter is that Americans, for example, are not exhorted by their proverbs to conform as Japanese are, so the quest for a perfect equivalent is probably doomed from the outset. It would be hard to find Japanese equivalents for some of the more puritanical of Anglo-American proverbs ("Spare the rod and spoil the child"), and Mr. Galef has perhaps not been entirely successful in finding an English equivalent for a very Buddhist one, *Ko wa sangai no kubikase* (no. 76), also about children.

I do not mean to reprove him. He has done his work well, as has his illustrator, Mr. Hashimoto. These little frustrations are, as I have said, inevitable, and they make the book more interesting. It is a likeable book, and it tells us much about Japan.

—Edward G. Seidensticker, 1986

Foreword

Even A Stone Buddha Can Talk

Proverbs are short pithy sayings that embody general truths. As such, they provoke us to consider the extent to which truth exists at all. Some of the proverbs here are straightforward; others are more rhetorically complex. Take the Japanese saying "The ocean does not choose its trash" (number 111). It has great resonance these days, since the degradation of our natural environment weighs more and more heavily upon our minds. Yet this fact about oceans is not the real point of the saying at all. This proverb uses this truth in a metaphorical way to establish another, less evident one. Like our oceans, which are utterly receptive to anything that wind and water bring to them, a generous soul is open to all those around him. By way of one truth, we reach another. But is the second truth really true?

Perhaps this masquerade is needed because "The ocean does not choose its trash" is an injunction. Perhaps we naturally resist the type of wisdom that asks us to wise up. Other proverbs are less moralizing and, therefore, rhetorically more simple. Consider "Water in a sleeping ear" (number 114). This saying does little more than describe a moment of total surprise. The Japanese say "*Nemimi ni mizu*" frequently in the sense that something is news to them. There is no inducement to action of any kind. The "general truth" of water in a sleeping ear seems to lie much more in the surprise of being suddenly wakened from a nap than in any kind of ideation that might follow. There is no second truth. "A carp on a cutting board" (133), a proverb that expresses total helplessness, is similar in this way.

What is true about these two different types of proverbs—those that incite and moralize and those that simply describe a situation—is that both are visually powerful. Both create an image that lingers in the mind by establishing a cognitive hook on which to hang an idea or two. Often the images are arresting—"To chew sand" (134) or "A fire from a kimono sleeve" (171). Their vividness forces us to entertain the truth in its particular situation and to remember its connection with experience. In other words, without seeing truth in a lived context, we come up empty. A *kotowaza* (or proverb) is meaningless unless we can do this. If there is no imagination, there is no truth.

This tendency to make meaning visual (and lyrical) is a fundamental feature of Japanese aesthetics. The propensity explains why, for instance, the brief lyricism of a thirty-one-syllable *waka* or a seventeen-syllable *haiku* can justify interpretation after interpretation, meaning after meaning, translation after translation, when they are often nothing more than a statement of observation. Here is just one famous example, loosely translated from Matsuo Bashō's *Journey to the Deep North*:

In the silence of the temple,
a cicada's voice
penetrates the rocks.

The proverbs contained in *Even a Stone Buddha Can Talk* share such brevity. Because of this, they similarly thirst for the visible context of their truth.

For the translator, brevity and its call for the situational nature of proverbial truth poses considerable problems. In David Galef's preface to the previous volume, *Even Monkeys Fall from Trees* (1987), he explains the rather complicated process that led to the features of that enjoyable book (which are repeated in this second volume). First, we start with a Japanese original; then comes a fairly literal translation of the proverb; then a Western equivalent of the same; and, finally, a graphic translation. "I felt continually that something was missing," he writes. "In attempting to describe the meaning of *Uma no mimi ni nembutsu* (A sutra in a horse's ear), I realized what it was I wanted: a slightly bored horse, perhaps wearing a sun-hat, being lectured to by a patient priest–in a word, illustration."

Jun Hashimoto has collaborated with Galef once again to make another one hundred Japanese proverbs come to life. They make a good pair. Whether word or figure, their work is true to the situational, experiential emphasis of Japanese aesthetics in general, and of proverbial wisdom in particular. Just as, say, the brief poems of *The Tale of Ise* require prose explanations of the particular moment that led to the creation of a particular poem, so, too, do Hashimoto's images make us consider the particular moment of the proverb, the truth of real life that generates wisdom.

Our attempt to imagine an actual moment of truth is, of course, the very pleasure of this book and, beyond this, a reason to applaud the continuing life of conventional wisdom. For no other form of writing makes us more curious about its provenance than the proverb. Who was it, for instance, who first stated the devastating truth, "You can't smell your own bad breath" (169)? Or what bad experience led someone to utter for the first time, "Blowfish is tasty, but life is precious" (151)?

Certainly, neither bad breath nor death by blowfish happened just once. We assume a repeatability of experience freed from the linearity of modern history and able to jump back over cultural borders, though there are exceptions, such as "Swimming on a dried mat" (124). In other words, one attractive quality of these pithy sayings is precisely the difficulty we would have in trying to imagine a single moment of their creation. To the extent that such a moment both escapes us and seems continually imaginable, the proverbs take on an attractive timelessness and even timelessness.

—Charles Shirō Inouye, 1999

Japanese Proverbs

1.

馬子にも衣装 *Mago ni mo ishō.*

Even a packhorse driver looks fine in proper dress.
[Clothes make the man.]

Packhorse drivers were the truckers of the pre-automotive world. As with other workaday jobs, the dress code was simple and rugged. Yet appearances count, and in fact the message of this proverb is optimistic: anyone can look like a gentleman.

2.

膝とも談合 *Hiza tomo dangō.*

Consult anyone, even your knees.
[Two heads are better than one.]

In a society where the group is far more important than the individual, seeking counsel is customary. Of course, this practice can be taken to comical extremes. Still, the belief persists that any consensus is stronger than one opinion.

3.

猿も木から落ちる *Saru mo ki kara ochiru.*

Even monkeys fall from trees.

[Anyone can make a mistake.]

Even the naturally graceful may slip at times. This proverb shows admiration for the gifted, matched with sympathy for those who make a mistake. The ancient Greco-Roman world had a saying, "Even Homer nods," parallel to *Kōbō ni mo fude no ayamari* (弘法にも筆の誤り): "Even Kōbō makes a mistake with his brush." (Kōbō Daishi [774–835] was a renowned calligrapher.)

4.

紺屋の白袴 *Kon'ya no shiro-bakama.*

Dyers wear undyed trousers.
[Shoemakers' children go barefoot.]

Everyone knows of a doctor who refuses medicine or a carpenter whose house is falling into ruin. One can be too busy professionally to attend to one's own needs. "Physician, heal thyself" represents such a sentiment.

5.

千里の道も一歩から *Sen-ri no michi mo ippo kara.*

Even a thousand-mile journey begins with the first step.
[Everyone has to start somewhere.]

This proverb stems from the Chinese philosopher Lao Tse: the importance of slow but steady progress in a spiritual quest. But it also reflects a practical truth, that one must conquer one's fear and take that necessary initial move. Consider the maxim "There's no time like the present."

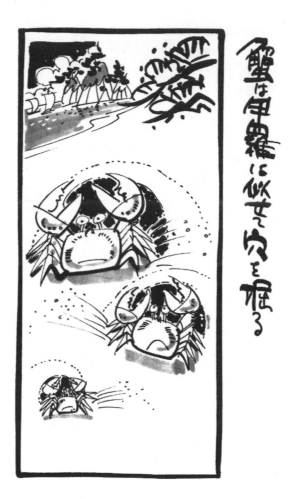

蟹は甲羅に似せて穴を掘る

6.

蟹は甲羅に似せて穴を掘る

Kani wa kōra ni nisete ana o horu.

Crabs dig holes according to the size of their shells.
[Cut your coat according to your cloth.]

Reflecting the natural world, proverbs such as this one establish a morality based on biology. As species act instinctively, people should act appropriately to their station—a very Japanese sentiment, though Americans say "Don't get too big for your britches." A related sentiment is *Bun sōō ni kaze ga fuku* (分相応に風が吹く): "The wind blows to each man according to his way of life."

7.

人生は風前の灯 *Jinsei wa fūzen no tomoshibi.*

Life is a candle light before the wind.

[Our life is but a span.]

The fragility and accidental loss of life is a lesson that every generation must learn. Existence is short and easily extinguished. Before and after are darkness. As the burial service in *The Book of Common Prayer* has it, "Ashes to ashes, dust to dust."

8.

蛇の道はへび *Ja no michi wa hebi.*

Snakes follow the way of serpents.
[Set a thief to catch a thief.]

Obviously about imitation, this proverb has a sinister aspect because snakes are often viewed as sly or evil. In short, this proverb is also about corruption. A gentler form of this observation about mimicry is "Monkey see, monkey do."

9.

戴く物は夏でも小袖 *Itadaku mono wa natsu de mo kosode.*

A padded jacket is an acceptable gift even in summer.
[Take what you can get.]

This proverb refers to a gift out of season—i.e., an inappropriate one. (A *kosode* is a short-sleeved garment, but quilted and hence worn in winter.) The point here is that such a gift is better than nothing—or at least so run the thoughts of a materialist.

同病相憐む

10.

同病相憐れむ *Dōbyō-ai awaremu.*

People with the same disease share sympathy.
[Misery loves company.]

Empathy, in this instance feeling another's pain, is easier when one is in the same boat, to use another proverbial expression. The phrase "birds of a feather" conveys a similar sense of shared qualities, but adversity in particular seems to create a bond.

11.

仏の顔も三度 *Hotoke no kao mo san-do.*

A Buddha's face when asked three times.

[Enough to try the patience of a saint.]

Though stoicism and patience are considered prime virtues in Japanese society, reflected in part by Buddhist tenets, everyone has a breaking point. See 101, *Ishibotoke mo mono o iu*: "Even a stone Buddha will say something."

一文惜しみの百損

12.

一文惜みの百損 *Ichi-mon oshimi no hyaku-zon.*

One coin saved, a hundred losses.

[Penny-wise, pound-foolish.]

This proverb is based on the uncomfortable realization that one can lose by trying too hard to gain. Note: In Old Japan, a *mon* was a cheap copper or iron coin. On a higher plain, as the Book of Mark in the Bible observes, "For what shall it profit a man, if he shall gain the whole world, and lose his own soul?"

13.

悪事千里を走る *Akuji sen-ri o hashiru.*

An evil act runs a thousand miles.

[Bad news travels fast.]

This saying stresses the talk generated by a bad deed rather than the act's evil effects. A country is sometimes as gossipy as a small village: an equivalent in the United States is "spreading like wildfire."

14.

郷に入っては郷に従え *Gō ni itte wa gō ni shitagae.*

Obey the customs of the village you enter.
[When in Rome, do as the Romans.]

This proverb is about conformity, requesting outsiders not to disrupt the society they're visiting. Though the "don't rock the boat" message may seem quintessentially Japanese, the equivalent ancient Roman maxim shows otherwise.

畑から蛤はとれぬ

15.

畑から蛤はとれぬ *Hatake kara hamaguri wa torenu.*

You can't get clams from a field.
[You can't get blood from a stone.]

Denying a request for something in the wrong season, this saying is as
fatalistic as it is practical. It also slyly indicts those with such ridiculous
aims. *Ki ni yorite uo o motomu*（木に縁りて魚を求む）from a Chinese
source, presents a similar impossibility: "to get fish from the trees."

16.

船頭多くして船山に登る

Sendō ōku shite fune yama ni noboru.

Too many boatmen will bring a boat up a mountain.
[Too many cooks spoil the broth.]

This common-sense proverb reflects the truth that two or more pieces of advice may be contradictory and result in misdirection. Though its spirit may run counter to the Japanese desire for consultation, it implicitly stresses another aspect of Japanese society: hierarchy.

17.

裏には裏がある　*Ura ni wa ura ga aru.*

The reverse side has its reverse side.
[There are wheels within wheels.]

Despite the Japanese emphasis on simplicity, this proverb makes a bid for complexity, along with a possible reference to the hidden face of subterfuge. On the other hand, it may also suggest tolerance: There is another side to every question.

18.

多芸は無芸 *Tagei wa mugei.*

Too many accomplishments make no accomplishment.
[Jack of all trades, master of none.]

Versatility is not a virtue prized much in Japanese society, nor in trade and the arts, where people make a reputation based on one specific skill or technique. This proverb is an indirect argument for specialization. See 27, *Mochi wa mochiya*: "For rice cakes, go to the rice-cake maker."

19.

口は災いの元 *Kuchi wa wazawai no moto.*

The mouth is the cause of calamity.
[The mouth is the gate of evil.]

Japanese society values taciturnity and discretion. Talking too much is viewed as irresponsible. Secrets may be betrayed, a universal worry. During World War II, for instance, the United States government adopted the slogan "Loose lips might sink ships" (the word "might" was later dropped).

20.

落下枝に帰らず、破鏡再び照らさず
Rakka eda ni kaerazu, hakyō futatabi terasazu.

Fallen blossoms do not return to branches; a broken mirror does not again reflect.

[There's no use crying over spilt milk.]

Herein lies the sad recognition that accidents happen, and the past cannot be undone. The more familiar Japanese proverb in this vein is *Fukusui bon ni kaerazu* (覆水盆に帰らず): "Spilled water does not return to the tray."

21.

鬼の女房鬼神がなる *Oni no nyōbō kijin ga naru.*

The wife of a devil grows worse than her mate.
[The apprentice outstrips the master.]

Imitation may be the sincerest form of flattery, and it may also lead to an intensified form of the original. Many are familiar with the zeal of a convert who outdoes the flock, though the transformation in this proverb is mainly negative.

卯と誓いは砕けやすい

22.

卵と誓いは砕けやすい *Tamago to chikai wa kudake-yasui.*

Eggs and vows are easily broken.
[Actions speak louder than words.]

This proverb is not well known, but its message is common. In a politeness society, people don't always say what they mean, and the truth is fragile. Perhaps more equivalent is the rough maxim "Talk is cheap," or the more practical but old-fashioned saying "Pudding before praise."

一杯は人酒を飲み　二杯は酒酒を飲み　三杯は酒人を飲む

23.

一杯は人酒を飲み、二杯は酒酒を飲み、三杯は酒人
を飲む　*Ippai wa hito sake o nomi, nihai wa sake sake o nomi,
sambai wa sake hito o nomu.*

**First the man takes a drink, then the drink takes a drink,
then the drink takes the man.**
[Wine is a mocker; strong drink is raging.]

Alcohol and its dangerous appeal are common subjects in folklore. This
proverb illustrates how the drinker loses control of his faculties, with a
cleverly phrased intermediate stage. The sober Western equivalent above
is from Proverbs 20.1 in the Bible.

24.

味噌の味噌臭いは上味噌にあらず
Miso no miso-kusai wa jō-miso ni arazu.

The bean paste that smells like bean paste is not the best quality.

[All that glitters is not gold.]

This rather obscure proverb may seem puzzling, particularly to any culture that values authenticity. In fact, it warns against what looks—or smells—too good to be true. It may also be a plea for subtlety and restraint. As the Latin phrase has it, *Ars est celarem artem*: "Art is to conceal art."

25.

一寸の虫にも五分の魂

Issun no mushi ni mo go-bu no tamashii.

Even a one-inch insect has a half-inch soul.

[Everything has its place.]

This Buddhist-inflected proverb notes the sacredness of all living creatures, with the understood message that they deserve our respect. The proverb is also quoted as a warning against reprisal, however: "Even a worm will turn."

26.

毛深い物は色深い *Ke-bukai mono wa iro-bukai.*

A hairy person is sexy.
[Bald and barren.]

Most Asian men have little body hair, so hirsute men are a curiosity. Even though that perspective doesn't hold true in Western society, hairless individuals anywhere are often seen as effete. Note: most Japanese readily understand this proverb, though it's not in general circulation.

餅は餅屋

27.

餅は餅屋 *Mochi wa mochiya.*

For rice cakes, go to the rice-cake maker.

[The right man for the right job.]

The emerging middle class in old Japan spawned a society of specialists that endures to this day, from the pickle-seller to the tofu-monger. Expertise in a trade is worth paying extra for, and one should stick to what one knows best.

28.

捕らぬ狸の皮算用　*Toranu tanuki no kawa-zan'yō.*

Don't estimate the value of a raccoon dog skin before catching the raccoon dog.

[Don't count your chickens before they're hatched.]

Every society warns against the danger of presumptuousness, of basing a future on plans that may not eventuate. Note: a *tanuki* or racoon dog is a species that's not quite a raccoon and not quite a badger.

泣く子と地頭には勝てぬ

29.

泣く子と地頭には勝てぬ *Naku ko to jitō ni wa katenu.*

**It is impossible to win over a crying child or
government officials.**

[You can't fight city hall.]

Japanese society is said to work by cooperation and consensus, but this
proverb establishes a parallel between two intransigent forces with which
there is no reasoning. The saying isn't anti-offspring so much as a dig
against government.

30.

犬も歩けば棒にあたる *Inu mo arukeba bō ni ataru.*

A dog that walks around will find a stick.
[Don't go looking for trouble. Or: Seek and ye shall find.]

This proverb originally cautioned against undue curiosity: poke your nose into too many places, and you'll get beaten. "Curiosity killed the cat." But more recent readings transform the meaning into the importance of taking initiative, with the stick changed into a reward for the dog.

31.

花より団子 *Hana yori dango.*

Dumplings are better than flowers.
[Pudding before praise.]

The notion that the Japanese are an austere, ascetic race is contradicted by a fair number of proverbs that emphasize creature comforts over aesthetics, at least at certain times. Other Japanese proverbs praise sake or lovemaking over blossoms.

32.

塵もつもれば山となる *Chiri mo tsumoreba yama to naru.*

Even dust amassed will grow into a mountain.

[Great oaks from little acorns grow.]

Industry and diligence are prized virtues in Japanese society, as is the idea that a little can slowly amount to a lot. The precept "Slow and steady wins the race" is comparable, as is 5: *Sen-ri no michi mo ippo kara*: "Even a thousand-mile journey begins with the first step."

33.

泣きっ面に蜂 *Nakittsura ni hachi.*

A bee stinging a crying face.
[Adding insult to injury.]

On a bad day, problems seem to pile up. Another way of expressing this idea is *Fundari kettari* (踏んだり蹴ったり): "to be trampled while kicked." Worse: one well-known Chinese proverb states that misfortunes come in threes.

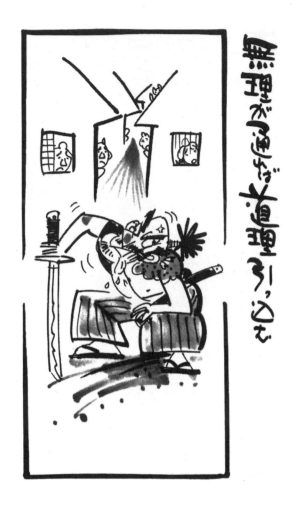

34.

無理が通れば道理引っ込む *Muri ga tōreba dōri hikkomu.*

When illogic prevails, reason gives way.
[Might makes right.]

This saying admits that sometimes "correct" thinking must yield to other, darker forces (it isn't a proverb praising love over logic). See 29, *Naku ko to jitō ni wa katenu*: "It is impossible to win over a crying child or government officials."

35.

臭い物に蓋 *Kusai mono ni futa.*

Put a lid on what smells bad.
[Don't wash dirty linen in public.]

The Japanese are known for their discretion, and more for *not* talking about a situation than talking about it. This proverb suggests active suppression, as in the Americanism "Put a lid on it."

36.

貧乏暇なし *Bimbō hima nashi.*

Poor people have no leisure.

[There is no rest for the weary.]

The sad observation behind this proverb suggests a different image from that of the carefree hobo in some stories. Everyone must work to make money, and if you're poor, you have to work more. On the other hand, this proverb is sometimes used as an excuse for not getting back to someone.

背に腹はかえられぬ

37.

背に腹はかえられぬ *Se ni hara wa kaerarenu.*

The back cannot take the place of the belly.
[Self-preservation is the first law of nature.]

This proverb is puzzling until one understands that the belly or *hara* is the spiritual center of the body; in a sense, its soul. The back is the source of protection, but only that. To prize the back would be like valuing one's armor over what it's supposed to defend.

38.

薮をつついて蛇を出す *Yabu o tsutsuite hebi o dasu.*

By poking at a bamboo thicket, one drives out a snake.
[Let sleeping dogs lie.]

Don't court trouble. The Japanese take pains to avoid causing a commotion and preserve the status quo. Don't poke around in others' business. See the first meaning of 30, *Inu mo arukeba bō ni ataru*: "A dog that walks around will find a stick."

39.

親しき仲にも礼儀あり *Shitashiki naka ni mo reigi ari.*

There are formalities between the closest of friends.
[Familiarity breeds contempt.]

Japanese society is all about deportment, from the proper honorifics to the correct degree of bowing. This state of affairs holds true even among people who know each other well. The Western saying about familiarity and contempt suggests the opposite view.

犬の喧嘩に子供が出、子供の喧嘩に親が出る

40.
犬の喧嘩に子供が出、子供の喧嘩に親が出る
Inu no kenka ni kodomo ga de, kodomo no kenka ni oya ga deru.
Dogfights draw children; children's fights draw parents.
[One thing leads to another.]

This semi-humorous proverb includes an escalation from the trivial to where authorities must intervene. It also suggests a nest of realms, of social causes and reactions, in increasing importance.

41.

絵に描いた餅は食えぬ *E ni kaita mochi wa kuenu.*

You can't eat the rice cake in a picture.
[Never confuse art with life.]

Japanese art tends to stylize nature, as in ocean waves or summer flowers painted on the side of a teacup. Still, art remains static, removed from reality. Therein lies its enchanting power—and capacity to frustrate.

蛙の子は蛙

42.

蛙の子は蛙 *Kaeru no ko wa kaeru.*

The child of a frog is a frog.
[Like father, like son.]

Every culture has observed that one's offspring tend to resemble one; hence, "the acorn doesn't fall far from the tree" or "a chip off the old block." What makes some proverbs seem Japanese is their use of insects, amphibians, and fish for metaphors.

43.

出る釘は打たれる *Deru kugi wa utareru.*

The protruding nail will be hammered.
[Don't make waves.]

This proverb is often cited as the quintessential statement about Japanese conformity, though certainly other cultures have similar warnings. On the other hand, it's hard to see "The squeaky wheel gets the grease" gaining much favor in Japan.

44.

馬鹿も一芸 *Baka mo ichi-gei.*

Even a fool has one talent.
[Even a broken clock is right twice a day.]

In village life, everyone can be put to some use, and to see the good in otherwise useless items—or in people—is particularly Japanese. Compare to 106, *Muyō no yō*: "A use for the useless."

45.

負けるが勝ち *Makeru ga kachi.*

To lose is to win.

[The race is not to the swift.]

Herein lies the Japanese belief that non-confrontation is the best course. Even the quintessential Japanese martial art, karate, means "empty hand." To quote another proverb in this vein: *Sanjūrokkei nigeru ni shikazu* (三十六計逃げるに如かず): "Thirty-six plans—fleeing is the best tactic."

46.

十人十色 *Jū-nin, to-iro.*

Ten men, ten tastes.

[There is no accounting for tastes.]

"Ten men, ten tastes" comes from the Chinese, but a Latin proverb says it just as well: *De gustibus non disputandum est*: "In taste, there can be no disputing."

47·

去る者は日々に疎し *Saru mono wa hibi ni utoshi.*

Those who depart are forgotten, day by day.

[Out of sight, out of mind.]

A seemingly callous saying, this proverb reflects the hard truth that impressions of others fade when not prompted by daily appearances. The Western equivalent, "Out of sight, out of mind," is from a line in a 16th-century sonnet by Fulke Greville: "And out of mind as soon as out of sight."

48.

地震、雷、火事、親父 *Jishin, kaminari, kaji, oyaji.*

Earthquakes, thunderbolts, fires, fathers.
[Fear those greater than yourself.]

A reverence—and fear—for natural phenomena is traditional in Japanese culture and probably universal. These forces have the potential for uncontrollable destruction. But the proverb's inclusion of the fourth term, fathers, lends a note both wry and sober.

爪の垢を煎じて飲む

49.

爪の垢を煎じて飲む *Tsume no aka o senjite nomu.*

Boil and drink another's fingernail dirt.
[To follow in someone's footsteps.]

To emulate another was how one succeeded as an apprentice or mastered a craft in traditional Japan. This proverb adds a seeming touch of voodoo, the idea of taking a small sample from someone to become that person.

京の夢、大阪の夢

50.

京の夢、大阪の夢 *Kyō no yume, Ōsaka no yume.*

Dreams in Kyoto, dreams in Osaka.

[Wishing will make it so.]

This saying was used in previous eras by people with big aspirations. Repeating these words signified a wish for one's dream to become reality. Kyoto, the capital during the Edo period, represented a hope for social success. Osaka, the commercial center, fed people's dreams for financial gain.

51.

旅は道ずれ世は情け *Tabi wa michizure, yo wa nasake.*

In traveling, a companion; in life, sympathy.
[A friend in need is a friend indeed.]

In old Japan, taking a trip was somewhat hazardous, and it was best to go accompanied. The larger idea, however, involves emotional support, with the metaphor of life as a journey.

52.

屁をひって尻つぼめ *He o hitte shiri tsubome.*

There is no use scrunching up your buttocks after a fart.
[No use shutting the barn door after the horse has bolted.]

Public embarrassment spurs the imagery in this proverb, which really
has to do with the futility of counteracting what one has already
set into motion. For all its seeming propriety, Japan has its share of
bathroom humor.

葦の髄から天井を見る

53.

葦の髄から天井を見る *Yoshi no zui kara tenjō o miru.*

One sees the sky through a hollow reed.
[Sometimes you can't see the forest for the trees.]

The image conveyed here is of a narrow or insular view, which is fitting, since Japan is an island nation and still has a reputation for being somewhat closed off. The proverb may also mean taking a long time for a task because of the smallness of the tool: emptying the sea with a spoon, or viewing the sky through a tube.

54.

三つ子の魂百まで *Mitsugo no tamashii hyaku made.*

The spirit of a three-year-old lasts a hundred years.
[The child is the father of the man.]

Here is another Buddhist-inspired maxim: preserving the nature of youth, its curiosity and freshness, into one's old age. A less flattering image of this idea is conveyed by *Kamu uma wa shimai made kamu* (噛む馬はしまいまで噛む): "A horse that bites will bite till the end."

55.

門前の小僧習わぬ経を読む

Monzen no kozō narawanu kyō o yomu.

A boy living near a Buddhist temple can learn an untaught sutra by heart.

[Experience is the best teacher.]

One learns from what's nearby and from what one hears over and over: proximity and repetition. Rote learning is still key in the Japanese educational system, but this saying makes education sound almost incidental and fun.

56.

急がば回れ *Isogaba maware.*

When in a hurry, take the roundabout route.
[The more haste, the less speed.]

Though the Japanese are not known for an emphasis on leisure, they are practical. Speeding up can lead to mistakes. Just as important in this proverb is that hurrying can lead to acting obliviously, and one notices more when on a leisurely path.

57.

念には念を入れよ *Nen ni wa, nen o ireyo.*

Add caution to caution.

[Look before you leap.]

Circumspection is a prime virtue in Japan, a land of checks and double-checks, as the repetition of *nen* ("care" or "attention") in this proverb makes clear. The saying *Ishibashi o tataite wataru* (石橋を 叩いて 渡る: "Rap on a stone bridge before crossing it") stresses this point.

58.

馬の耳に念仏 *Uma no mimi ni nembutsu.*

A sutra in a horse's ear.
[Preaching to deaf ears.]

Of the many universal proverbs describing wasted efforts, a fair
proportion seem connected to horses, as in "Like flogging a dead horse."
This particular proverb also presents the image of an inappropriate,
unresponsive audience, as in *Baji tōfu* (馬耳東風): an east wind (a
favorable omen) in the ear of a horse.

59.

吝ん坊の柿の種 *Shiwambō no kaki no tane.*

A miser and his persimmon seeds.

[A penny pincher will pick up anything.]

This proverb neatly sums up the impulse behind greed, in this instance an obsession to hoard anything, even dried-up seeds, no longer connected to the fruit itself.

60.

頭隠して尻隠さず *Atama kakushite shiri kakusazu.*

One hides the head and leaves the rear end uncovered.
[Protect yourself at all points.]

This warning is as applicable to battle as it is to rising up the ranks of a corporate ladder: don't leave yourself vulnerable. The image is that of an ostrich, who thinks it's safe when it buries its head in the sand and can no longer see the danger.

61.

善は急げ *Zen wa isoge.*

Do quickly what is good.
[Strike while the iron is hot.]

Timing matters, especially in the performance of admirable deeds. "Make hay while the sun shines" is another Western equivalent—in a sense the opposite of 56: *Isogaba maware*: "When in haste, take the roundabout route," or "Look before you leap."

62.

年寄りの冷や水 *Toshiyori no hiyamizu.*

An old man dips into cold water.
[There's no fool like an old fool.]

Despite a real reverence for elders, the Japanese also have an aversion to senility and eccentricities. To brave frigid water when one is old is unwise, even if the attempt is to show courage.

63.

身から出た錆 *Mi kara deta sabi.*

Rust comes from within the body.
[As you make your bed, so you must lie in it.]

"You have only yourself to blame" runs the meaning of this curiously worded proverb, yet with the added meaning of infirmity and the image of the self as an iron figure. The Biblical version is "As you sow, so shall ye reap."

64.

大魚は小池に棲まず *Taigyo wa shōchi ni sumazu.*

Big fish do not live in small ponds.
[A great ship must have deep water.]

That significant people are usually found in important places rather than backwaters is a common observation, though the emphasis here on appropriateness and proportionality is particularly Japanese, as is the image of a fish.

65.

恋と咳とは隠されぬ *Koi to seki to wa kakusarenu.*

Love and a cough cannot be hidden.
[Love conquers all.]

Though the Japanese tend not to wear their hearts on their sleeves, no society denies the uncontrollable nature of love. Significantly, though, love is placed on the level of an indiscretion or an infirmity.

66.

運は勇者を助く　*Un wa yūsha o tasuku.*

Fate aids the courageous.
[Fortune favors the brave.]

Destiny may be inexorable, but those who show a plucky spirit seem somehow favored by the gods. This sentiment is distinct from the destiny-driven maxim *Un wa ten ni ari* (運は天にあり): "Our fate is in heaven."

67.

昔とった杵柄 *Mukashi totta kinezuka.*

The skill of using a mortar and pestle never leaves one.
[You never forget your own trade.]

Though this proverb refers to pounding rice or grain (a *kinezuka* is a long-handled pestle), the meaning refers to any learned activity. As Westerners say, "It's like riding a bike: you never forget how."

骨折り損のくたびれ儲け

68.

骨折り損のくたびれ儲け *Hone ori-zon no kutabire mōke.*
Break your bones and earn only exhaustion.
[Much pain, little gain.]

Though the Japanese are great believers in hard work, this proverb runs somewhat counter to the social ethos, tapping into a fatalistic view of life. Sometimes all the effort in the world accomplishes nothing, or, as the Japanese say with a shrug, *Shikata ga nai* (仕方がない): "It can't be helped."

果報は寝て待て

69.

果報は寝て待て *Kahō wa nete mate.*

Sleep and wait for good luck.

[Everything comes to him who waits.]

For all that Japanese society seems to run on no-nonsense communal effort, a superstitious element persists, and this aspect, aligned with the virtue of patience, makes for this proverb.

70.

柳の下にいつも鰌はいない

Yanagi no shita ni itsu-mo dojō wa inai.

One cannot always find a fish under a willow.

[No one's luck lasts forever.]

This proverb is in keeping with the Japanese disdain for those who depend on the whims of chance. Note: a *dojō* is a loach, a small freshwater fish.

71.

老いては子に従え *Oite wa ko ni shitagae.*

When you grow old, obey your children.
[The old must make way for the new.]

Despite their respect for the aged, the Japanese are also utilitarian. Traditionally, the Japanese often lived with their parents or in-laws, who had a strong say in family life. But when one has grown so old that one is no longer in authority, it's time to heed the voice of one's offspring.

72.
能ある鷹は爪を隠す *Nō aru taka wa tsume o kakusu.*

A clever hawk hides its claws.
[He who knows most speaks least.]

This proverb is firmly in line with the Japanese sense of modesty. Those with skills don't boast about them, and ostentatious displays may scare off whomever one hopes to attract. As the Western saying runs, "Actions speak louder than words."

73.

珍客も長座に過ぎれば厭われる

Chinkyaku mo chōza ni sugireba itowareru.

Even a welcome guest becomes tiresome by overstaying.
[Fish and visitors stink in three days.]

The lavish hospitality in Japan is balanced by a sense of decorum. Precisely because the Japanese go to such lengths to make others feel at home, guests shouldn't take advantage of their hosts. Note: when a Japanese host offers tea, that's usually a sign that it's time to leave.

74.

八十の手習い *Hachijū no tenarai.*

One may study calligraphy at eighty.
[It's never too late to learn.]

When Japanese retire, they often take up traditional arts, such as calligraphy or the tea ceremony. This optimistic saying is the opposite of "You can't teach an old dog new tricks." Note: a variant of this proverb stipulates sixty rather than eighty years. See 112, *Taiki bansei*: "Genius matures late."

残り物に福があり

75.

残り物に福があり　*Nokorimono ni fuku ga ari.*

The leftover piece is lucky.

[Last but not least.]

This saying conveys the opposite of the phrase *Enryo no kata mari* (遠慮の固まり): a polite hesitation over taking the last piece. By extension, the proverb acknowledges that being last may be special rather than a disgrace.

子は三界の首枷

76.

子は三界の首枷 *Ko wa sangai no kubikase.*

Children yoke parents to the past, present, and future.
[Children are a burden to their parents.]

Having offspring certainly makes one sensitive to time in all frames, from heritage to posterity. Often this awareness is positive, but *kubikase* is a yoke or shackle, making the connotation negative.

良薬は口に苦し

77.

良薬は口に苦し　*Ryōyaku wa kuchi ni nigashi.*

Good medicine tastes bitter in the mouth.

[Advice when most needed is least heeded.]

This proverb stresses a willingness to endure something hard to bear in order to gain good results, while recognizing that few people care for such trials—even if "The ends justify the means."

腐れ縄も役に立つ

78.

腐れ縄も役に立つ *Kusare-nawa mo yaku ni tatsu.*

Even a rotting rope can be put to use.

[Necessity is the mother of invention.]

The image presented is of ingenuity, particularly with unpromising materials. For instance, *chadō*, the Japanese tea ceremony, creates a whole world of aesthetics and discipline from a few tea utensils and hot water.

79.
八方美人は薄情 *Happō bijin wa hakujō.*
An eight-sided beauty is cold-hearted.
[Fair and fickle.]

Herein is the common division between inward and outward appeal, or of appearance versus true worth. Implied is the notion that too much external appeal makes for a shallow interior. Note: the eight sides derive from the image of compass directions.

身を殺して仁をなす

80.

身を殺して仁をなす *Mi o koroshite jin o nasu.*

One becomes virtuous by subduing the body.
[The world, the flesh, and the devil.]

Zen austerity is similar to other strains of religious asceticism, from fasting and frugality to staying awake and ignoring bodily complaints. Note: the verb *korosu* in the proverb's "*koroshite*" means to kill, as well as subdue or put down.

他人の疝気を頭痛に病む

81.

他人の疝気を頭痛に病む *Tanin no senki o zutsū ni yamu.*

Don't get a headache over another's lumbago.

[Don't meddle in others' affairs.]

This proverb's phrasing, not to grow ill over another's infirmity, might seem callous, but it may also mean to choose what's significant; i.e., "Don't sweat the small stuff." Compare to 186, *Jibun no atama no hae o oe*: "Brush the flies away from your own head."

82.

柳に風 *Yanagi ni kaze.*

A willow before the wind.
[Follow the path of least resistance.]

This famous proverb, suggesting bending rather than breaking, exists in
part because Japan is not a society of whiners or troublemakers, but also
because conformity is preferable to fighting back. The message is in fact
universal. In Aesop's fables, the willow survives the tempest while the
oak is felled by the wind.

83.

短期は損気 *Tanki wa sonki.*

A short temper is a disadvantage.
[Be slow to anger, quick to befriend.]

Here is another Japanese proverb with an insistence on not getting emotional. Anger or "a short fuse" is harmful to everyday transactions, and Japanese society suggests suppressing displays of temper.

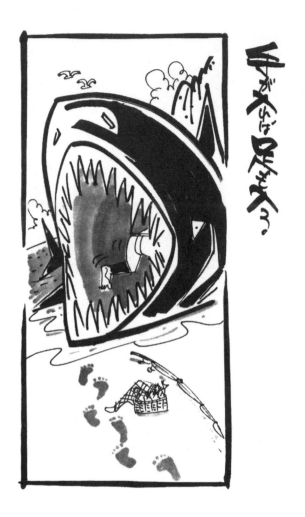

84.

手が入れば足も入る *Te ga ireba ashi mo iru.*

When the hand is put in, the foot follows.
[Draw back while there is still time.]

This proverb displays a reticence about commitment, with an ominous sense of being slowly swallowed up. The Western sentiment is well expressed by "Give them an inch, and they'll take a mile" (see 188, *Hisashi o kashite omoya o torareru*: "Lend the eaves and the main building will be taken").

鳥なき里の蝙蝠

85.

鳥なき里の蝙蝠 *Tori naki sato no kōmori.*

Like a bat in a birdless village.
[Like a one-eyed man in the kingdom of the blind.]

There is an advantage in a situation where one may not be so able but still the best in the bunch. Presumably, a bat is a poor model of a bird. As in the liveliest proverbs, the image comes from nature and village life.

86.

弁慶の泣き所 *Benkei no naki-dokoro.*

The spot that makes the warrior Benkei cry.
[Everyone has his Achilles' heel.]

This proverb is a recognition that everyone's human and vulnerable; at the same time, it is also a tactical observation that there's always a way to get at someone's weak spot.

87.

案ずるより産むが易し *Anzuru yori umu ga yasushi.*

Childbirth is easier than the worrying beforehand.
[It's always darkest before the dawn.]

Anxiety over giving birth is the metaphor here for what is in the larger sense a maxim about unnecessary fretting before an event happens. Despite the pain, the result is a joy.

虎穴に入らずんば虎児を得ず

88.

虎穴に入らずんば虎児を得ず
Koketsu ni irazumba koji o ezu.

You cannot catch a tiger cub unless you enter the tiger's den.
[Nothing ventured, nothing gained.]

Without being contradictory, the Japanese are both cautious and brave. This saying is a lesson in expediency and risk-taking: one must court danger to succeed in certain ventures.

89.

香を盗む物は香に現わる

Kō o nusumu mono wa kō ni arawaru.

He who steals incense smells of it.

[Guilt will out.]

Here is the aligning of a deed and its consequence, in this instance what one takes unlawfully. A Westerner might say, "The crime is written on his face."

90.

商売は草の種 *Shōbai wa kusa no tane.*

There are as many ways of making a living as seeds of grass.
[Each to his own trade.]

One of the many "world so wide" sayings in myriad cultures: there are innumerable ways of making a living on this earth. In a sense, this proverb is also a plea for diversity.

大食腹に満れば学問腹に入らず

91.

大食腹に満れば学問腹に入らず *Taishoku hara ni mitsureba gakumon hara ni irazu.*

A full belly is not the stomach of a scholar.
[Hunger sharpens the mind.]

This saying trades on the traditional image of the learned man who spends his little money on books rather than on food. In fact, "One cannot study on a full stomach" is another possible translation. For an opposed sentiment, consider *Hara ga hette wa ikusa wa dekinu* (腹が減っては戦ができぬ): "You can't fight on an empty stomach."

92.

丹漆飾らず *Tanshitsu kazarazu.*

A red lacquer dish needs no decoration.
[Beauty alone is sufficient.]

The image depends on the elegant simplicity in so much of Japanese art. Note: lacquer, derived from the toxic sap of the Japanese sumac tree, is applied in layers for a smooth, even surface, after which it may be carved or left as is.

臍を噛めども及ばぬ

93.

臍を噛めども及ばぬ *Heso o kamedomo oyobanu.*

It's no good trying to bite your navel.
[Don't cut off your nose to spite your face.]

This proverb presents an image of not just contortion, such as trying to stick one's elbow in one's ear, but also an action intended to get back at oneself. The maneuver is as ill-advised as it is physically impossible.

生兵法は大怪我の元

94.

生兵法は大怪我の元 *Nama-byōhō wa ō-kega no moto.*

Crude military tactics are the cause of severe casualties.
[A little learning is a dangerous thing.]

Finesse is key even in brute physicality. The use of force, how and when to apply it, is a much-discussed topic in *The Art of War*, by Sun Tzu, a Chinese army commander who lived around the time of Confucius and who is still influential today.

95.

京の着倒れ、大阪の食い倒れ

Kyō no kidaore, Ōsaka no kuidaore.

Kyoto people ruin themselves for clothing, Osaka people for food.

[Each goes to hell in his own way.]

Just as the city of Kyoto has long held a reputation for fashion, the city of Osaka is famous for entertainment. Note: *taoreru,* or *-daoreru* in compound, means to collapse—in this instance, from overdoing it.

96.

武士は食わねど高楊枝 *Bushi wa kuwanedo taka-yōji.*

Even when a samurai has not eaten, he holds his toothpick high.

[One must put on a brave display even in adversity.]

Bushidō, or the way of the warrior, is a code as chivalric as that of the knights at King Arthur's round table, emphasizing both courage and dignity. More generally, this proverb refers to holding one's head up, despite dispiriting circumstances.

97.

天に向かって唾を吐く *Ten ni mukatte tsuba o haku.*

The spit aimed at the sky comes back to one.
[Don't spit into the wind.]

This proverb graphically details actions and their consequences, of which the Japanese are exquisitely mindful. In the U.S. vernacular, people talk about how "what goes around comes around" and also refer to the boomerang effect.

98.

国滅びて山河あり *Kuni horobite sanga ari.*

Destroy a country, but its mountains and rivers remain.
[The land outlasts the king.]

This saying comes from a famous Chinese poem, referring to what's left even after military devastation. The faith in nature over manmade structures is particularly Asian.

99.

一寸先は闇 *Issun saki wa yami.*

Darkness lies one inch ahead.

[No man knows his own future.]

The Japanese can be at times fatalistic: life may be determined, even if it is to us indeterminable. *Issun,* or one *sun,* is a small unit of measurement, about 1.2 inches.

七転び八起き

100.

七転び八起き *Nana-korobi ya-oki.*

Fall down seven times, get up eight.
[If at first you don't succeed, try, try again.]

This proverb displays the determination that is the hallmark of Japanese culture. *Ganbatte* (がんばって): the exhortation heard before every sporting contest, exam, or other ordeal, can be translated as "good luck" but really means "persevere."

101.

石仏も物を言う *Ishibotoke mo mono o iu.*

Even a stone Buddha will say something.
[Enough to try the patience of a saint.]

There comes a time when even the most recalcitrant, or least likely to respond, answers back. This response may come from sheer urgency or other provocation, but it comes as a shock to others. The Japanese tendency toward taciturnity is evident here. Cf. 11, *Hotoke no kao mo san-do*: "A Buddha's face when asked three times."

102.

獅子身中の虫 *Shishi shinchū no mushi.*

Worms in the middle of a lion's body.
[Nourishing a snake in one's bosom.]

This proverb, which depends on images of decay and rebirth, is in fact a saying about hosting an evil presence within one's perimeter, of misplaced trust. A reflection of this concept is *On o ada de kaesu* (恩を仇で返す): "Return good with evil."

103.

手者より無者が怖い *Tesha yori nasha ga kowai.*

A person with nothing is more fearsome than one with talent.
[Fear the man who has nothing left to lose.]

This rarely used saying involves the power of desperation. People who have skills (or wealth or food) may be less inclined to attack than those who are well off. Caesar's fear of lean and hungry men in Shakespeare's *Julius Caesar* is relevant here.

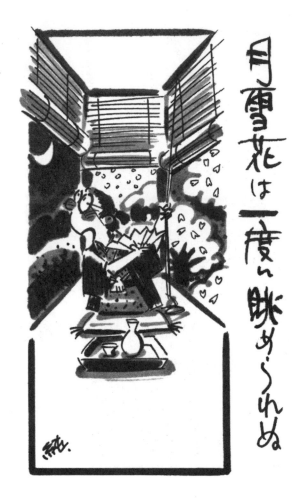

104.

月雪花は一度に眺められぬ

Tsuki yuki hana wa ichido ni nagamerarenu.

The moon, snow, and flowers cannot all be viewed at the same time.

[To everything there is a season.]

The Japanese regard a fresh snowfall, a full moon, and pretty flowers as aesthetic experiences in themselves. This remark conveys a lesson about greed or craving everything at once, or just the recognition that one can't have it all. Snow and flowers appear in different seasons, and flowers don't open at night, when the moon is out.

105.

長口上は欠伸の種 *Nagakōjō wa akubi no tane.*

A long speech is the source of yawns.
[Brevity is the soul of wit.]

Despite the length of formal speeches at Japanese ceremonies, terseness is a Japanese virtue; prolixity is frowned upon. In fact, many oral outpourings are viewed with suspicion in proverbs. Compare to 19, *Kuchi wa wazawai no moto*: "The mouth is the cause of calamity."

106.

無用の用 *Muyō no yō.*

A use for the useless.

[One man's trash is another man's treasure.]

This saying is both compassionate and practical. It also seems applicable to village life, where everyone matters in some way. Compare to 44. *Baka mo ichi-gei*: "Even a fool has one talent." Seen another way, this proverb may also seem greedy in using up everything: "All is grist for the mill."

身代につるる心

107.

身代につるる心 *Shindai ni tsururu-kokoro.*

Hanging one's heart on wealth.
[Money isn't everything.]

The image here, to pin everything on riches, involves the heart, though it's not an approving message. In fact, the underlying, spiritual idea is the reverse of what's stated: *don't* make money your master.

108.

死んだ子の年を数える *Shindako no toshi o kazoeru.*

Counting a dead child's years.

[A fruitless endeavor.]

This poignant proverb reflects the high mortality rate in old Japan, but also shows the human tendency to reflect on what might have been. Any parent hearing this phrase is bound to feel a pang. Compare to *Fuku sui bon ni kaerazu* (覆水盆に帰らず): "Spilled water does not return to the tray."

109.

猫に小判 *Neko ni koban.*

A gold coin to a cat.

[Pearls before swine.]

Appropriateness is a chief concern in Japan, epitomized here by how an object of value is wasted on some. But the sentiment is universal. See Matthew 7.6 in the Bible: "Give not that which is holy unto the dogs, neither cast ye your pearls before swine." *Buta ni shinju* (豚に真珠): "pearls to swine" is well known in Japan.

110.

礼も過ぎれば無礼になる *Rei mo sugireba burei ni naru.*

Exceeding courtesy becomes rudeness.
[Killing with kindness.]

This observation is particularly true in Japanese society, where an argument can start in plain speech and grow icily polite as it progresses. Like so many social paradoxes, it's built on the effect of excess. *Ingin burei* (慇懃無礼), "polite rudeness," is defined as condescension.

III.

大海は芥を択ばず *Taikai wa akuta o erabazu.*

The ocean does not choose its trash.

[A generous soul accepts everyone.]

This proverb seems to have a modern ecological tone, but its general message has to do with the almost incidental kindness of inclusion, and how it helps build a mighty whole. In the same spirit is *Taizan wa dojō o yuzurazu* (泰山は土壌を譲らず): "A high mountain does not give up any soil."

112.

大器晩成 *Taiki bansei.*

Genius matures late.

[Last but not least.]

This saying comes from the Chinese Lao Tse, but it applies equally well to traditional Japanese society, which placed less emphasis on youth than on the accumulation of age and what it could accomplish. Compare to 74, *Hachijū no tenarai*: "One may study calligraphy at eighty."

113.

善き分別は雪隠で出る *Yoki funbetsu wa setchin de deru.*

Wise judgment comes when on the toilet.
[Inspiration strikes in the unlikeliest of places.]

The Japanese tradition of meditation comes in part from Chinese
Buddhism. *Zazen* (座禅), or seated Zen contemplation, is probably
not best accomplished in the lavatory (another reading for *setchin*), but
what's important is the attitude, not the location. Note: this proverb is
not used much.

114.

寝耳に水 *Nemimi ni mizu.*

Water in a sleeping ear.
[A shock to the system.]

How best to startle someone is debatable, but this proverbial expression suggests the image of someone oblivious (*nemimi*: "sleeping ear"), abruptly and rudely woken. Whether the source is a drip in an old roof, a bucket of ice-water, or just some startling news, is immaterial.

死に馬に、鍼をさう

115.

死に馬に針を刺す *Shini uma ni hari o sasu.*

To stick needles in a dead horse.
[Like flogging a dead horse.]

Many proverbs present images of futility; compare to 108, *Shindako no toshi o kazoeru*: "Counting a dead child's years." In this instance, the attempted recovery, pricking the hide of the horse for a response or trying acupuncture, comes too late. It is a *muda-bone* (無駄骨), a useless endeavor.

116.

臍で茶を沸かす *Heso de cha o wakasu.*

To boil tea on one's navel.
[A belly laugh.]

This proverbial anatomical phrase makes for a wonderful image, despite its improbability, which is why figurative language is often so delightful. The underlying idea involves teasing or laughing at the expense of someone trying to do the impossible.

117.

憎まれっ子世にはばかる *Nikkumarekko yo ni habakaru.*

The hateful child does as he pleases in the world.
[Evil men flourish like the green bay tree.]

This proverb isn't anti-child but rather a glum acknowledgment that
the bad guy gets his way. It doesn't endorse such behavior. Rather, one
who's properly brought up does *not* do just as he wishes but instead is
conscious of others' needs and tries to fit in with the group.

118.

瑠璃も玻璃も照らせば光る

Ruri mo hari mo teraseba hikaru.

Emeralds and crystals glitter when lit.

[Encouragement brings out the best in people.]

Taking its cue from two types of rock that need light to sparkle, this proverb emphasizes the importance of giving a boost. Creating the proper environment makes individuals shine. Another interpretation is that talented individuals will shine no matter where.

119.

喉元過ぎれば熱さを忘れる

Nodomoto sugireba atsusa o wasureru.

Once past the throat, hot liquid is forgotten.

[Out of sight, out of mind.]

Memory of pain is short-lived, runs the message of this saying. Other proverbs detail the transiency of memory in general (see 47, *Saru mono wa hibi ni utoshi*: "Those who depart are forgotten, day by day"), whereas some suggest that one never forgets (see 67, *Mukashi totta kinezuka*: "The skill of using a mortar and pestle never leaves one").

120.

聞いて極楽見て地獄 *Kiite gokuraku mite jigoku.*

Hearing heaven, seeing hell.

[Imagination goes a long way.]

So many proverbs concern the split between appearance and reality, often between beauty and lack of virtue, or when something seems simply too good to be true. But people tend to deceive themselves, even when the ocular proof is right in front of them.

121.

楽は苦の種、苦は楽の種

Raku wa ku no tane, ku wa raku no tane.

Pleasure is the source of pain; pain is the source of pleasure.

[You have to take the rough with the smooth.]

The idea behind this maxim is both Buddhist—things of this world that delight also cause sorrow—and psychological—true joy comes only after some hardship is overcome, and pleasing experiences are often followed by a letdown. In other words, *Kafuku wa azanaeru nawa no gotoshi* (禍福はあざなえる縄の如し): "Good and bad luck are twisted together like rope strands."

転ばぬ先の杖

122.

転ばぬ先の杖 *Korobanu saki no tsue.*

A cane before falling.
[Better safe than sorry.]

The image behind this reflection on safety concerns the unsure footing of age, but the message is general: take precautions. As signs all over Japan read: *Anzen dai-ichi* (安全第一): "Safety first." The Boy Scouts' creed, "Be prepared," is equally relevant. Cf. 57, *Nen ni wa, nen o ireyo*: "Add caution to caution."

ただより高いものはない

123.

ただより高いものはない *Tada yori takai mono wa nai.*

There is nothing more costly than what's free.
[There's no such thing as a free lunch. (Or: You get what you pay for.)]

This saying embodies a cynical, if sometimes deserved, attitude toward whatever is gratis: it may have hidden costs, such as an obligation, known in Japanese as *giri.* "Looking a gift horse in the mouth" (checking its teeth for wear) shows that many people suspect what's free. "The best things in life are free" represents the opposite sentiment.

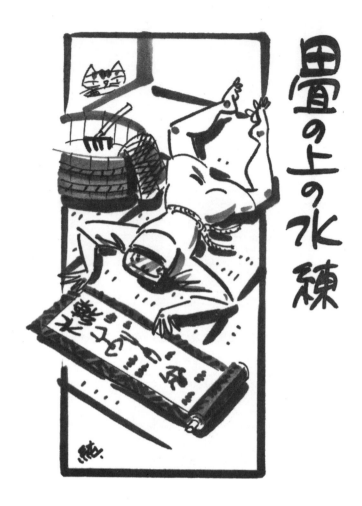

I 2 4.

畳の上の水練　*Tatami no ue no suiren.*

Training to swim on the tatami.
[Knowledge alone will get you only so far.]

Though this proverbial phrase may seem to stress the importance of making a dry run, in fact it shows how book-learning can fall short in tackling the real world. Practicing the breast stroke on a straw mat is no substitute for jumping into a lake. See *Kijō no kūron* (机上の空論): "armchair theory."

125.

四角な座敷を丸く掃く *Shikaku na zashiki o maruku haku.*

To sweep a four-cornered room in a circle.
[To cut corners, or: to do things by halves.]

Though the Japanese are known for their fastidious cleanliness, everyone takes shortcuts from time to time. Even the best-swept house may have a few dusty areas. The opposite impulse, paying too much attention to detail-work, is summed up in *Jūbako no sumi o yōji de hojikuru* (重箱の隅を楊枝でほじくる): "To stick a toothpick into the corners of a nested tier of boxes."

126.

職が敵 *Shoku gataki.*

Work-enemies.
[Two of a trade don't get along.]

Rivalries are universal but particularly common among those who practice the same profession. People tend to get annoyed at others in the same line of work who aren't quite the same as them; hence, this proverbial expression.

目は口程に物を言う

127.

目は口程に物を言う *Me wa kuchi hodo ni mono o iu.*

The eyes speak as well as the mouth.
[The eyes are the windows of the soul.]

This proverb describes expressiveness, especially in features that don't rely on words. *Me wa kokoro no kagami* (目は心の鏡), "The eyes are the mirror of the heart," represents this sentiment, as well.

128.

盗人と智者の相は同じ *Nusubito to chisha no sō wa onaji.*

Thieves and scholars look the same.

[You can't judge a book by its cover.]

The idea that a burglar may resemble a sage seems outrageous, but the point is that one cannot tell much from appearances or casual behavior. To quote a Western proverb: "All cats look gray in the dark."

129.

月夜に米の飯 *Tsuki-yo ni kome no meshi.*

A meal of rice under the evening moon.
[The simple things in life.]

The Japanese have an aesthetics based on simplicity, as the tea ceremony demonstrates. Here, a plain dish of food and an everyday setting is enough to stir pleasure. To some extent, the lines resemble Edward FitzGerald's English translation from Omar Khayyam's *Rubaiyat*: "A Jug of Wine, a Loaf of Bread—and Thou . . . ."

130.

水魚の交わり *Suigyo no majiwari.*

The mingling of water and fish.

[As a fish takes to water.]

This expression of Chinese origin conveys what goes together naturally, the theme depending on a favorite image: fish, which feature in so many Japanese proverbs. But the proverb is used most often to describe human relations: friends or spouses, for instance.

131.

亢龍悔い有り　*Kōryō kui ari.*

An exalted dragon suffers hardship.
[The bigger they are, the harder they fall.]

As magnificent, magical beasts, dragons often symbolize greatness in Asian art, but power and majesty are vulnerable to being unseated. As Proverbs 16.18 in the Bible declares, "Pride goeth before destruction, and an haughty spirit before a fall" (usually shortened to "Pride goeth before a fall"). Similarly, *Ogoru heike wa hisashi karazu* (驕る平家は久しからず): "The haughty Heike clan do not last long."

132.

盗み食いはうまい *Nusumi-gui wa umai.*

Stolen food is tasty.
[Stolen cherries are sweeter.]

Behind this saying is a nasty truth, that snatching something for free
sometimes give it an illicit thrill. In short, ill-gotten gains are especially
savored.

俎板の鯉

133.

俎板の鯉 *Manaita no koi.*

A carp on a cutting board.
[A lamb to the slaughter.]

This proverbial image aptly sums up the plight of a fish about to be hacked apart; by extension, anyone who feels sacrificial, helpless, or doomed. But another view of this expression is of accepting one's fate with equanimity, even courage.

I34.

砂を嚙む *Suna o kamu.*

To chew sand.
[To chew the carpet.]

The faces of enraged people are often contorted, their jaws moving silently. The corresponding image, biting something not meant to be eaten, conveys both anger and futility. The underlying frustration is that of masticating something that Westerners would term "as tasteless as sawdust." Note that this expression is more phrase than proverb, and not all that common.

135.

情けに刃向かう刃なし *Nasake ni hamukau yaiba nashi.*

No sword can oppose kindness.
[You catch more flies with honey than with vinegar.]

Herein lies the preference for a gentle approach rather than violence, a common theme in proverbial wisdom. Also along these lines is *Jinsha wa teki nashi* (仁者は敵なし) : "A kind person has no enemies."

136.

一条の矢は折べく十条は折べからず

Ichijō no ya wa orubeku, jūjō wa orubekarazu.

One arrow can easily break; ten arrows do not easily break.

[There is strength in numbers.]

Though this proverb applies to military forces as well as to mass opinion, the appeal to conformity, to a like-minded group rather than an individual, is also implied.

137.

話し上手の聞き下手 *Hanashi-jozu no kiki-beta.*

Good at talking, bad at listening.

[None so deaf as those who will not hear.]

The Japanese emphasis on deference is evident here, critical of those who pay no attention to anyone but themselves. Two old-fashioned Western directives to children, "Speak only when spoken to" and "Children should be seen and not heard," underscore this idea.

138.

ぼろを着ても心は錦 *Boro o kite mo kokoro wa nishiki.*

Though he wears rags, his heart is brocade.

[Beneath that rough exterior beats a heart of gold.]

This proverb is another illustration of the divide between appearance and reality, in a sense the mirror of 1, *Mago ni mi ishō*: "Even a packhorse driver looks fine in proper dress." The beloved Japanese film character Tora-san illustrates this proverb well: a simple man with a large heart.

善なるもの必ず美ならず

139.

善なるもの必ず美ならず

Zen naru mono kanarazu bi narazu.

What becomes good does not necessarily become beautiful.

[Beauty is only skin deep.]

Yet another lesson in appearance versus reality: here, a distinction between what is pleasing to the soul versus what is pleasing to the eye. The sense of transformation in *naru*, "to become," is apparent, but change does not work on all levels.

鵜の真似をする烏水に溺れる

140.

鵜の真似をする烏水に溺れる

U no mane o suru karasu, mizu ni oboreru.

A crow imitating a cormorant drowns in the water.

[To thine own self be true.]

This proverb is in a familiar vein, a warning against over-ambition. Taking on another's habits without the other's powers may be fatal. A crow cannot swim, so it shouldn't dive for fish as a cormorant does.

141.

早く熟すれば早く腐る　*Hayaku jukusureba hayaku kusaru.*

If it ripens quickly, it rots quickly.
[Easy come, easy go.]

The Japanese are particularly sensitive to anything short-lived; hence, their adoration for cherry blossoms, which emerge in a riot of bloom in April and soon carpet the ground. Shortly beyond fruition is decay.

142.

盲蛇に怖じず *Mekura hebi ni ojizu.*

The blind do not fear snakes.

[Ignorance is bliss.]

This proverb turns infirmity or adversity into a positive attribute, though perhaps one shouldn't pursue the consequences of the image: snakes may bite the blind and the seeing, the fearless and the cautious.

143.

学問に近道なし *Gakumon ni chikamichi nashi.*

There is no shortcut to scholarship.

[There is no royal road to learning.]

This saying stresses the necessity for hard work in any field, even though reading isn't the same as manual labor. An alternate reading for *gakumon* is simply "learning," and a variant of the proverb itself substitutes *ōdō* (王道) or "royal road" in place of *chikamichi*, "shortcut."

144.

敵に塩を贈る *Teki ni shio o okuru.*

Send salt to your enemy.

[Return good for evil.]

The ancient world valued salt as a commodity so much that the word *salary* derives from payment in salt. This saying is based on Japanese history: the 16th-century warlord Uesugi Kenshin, who sent salt to his adversary, Takeda Shingen, so they could keep on fighting. "Keep your friends close, but your enemies closer."

145.

有る一文無い千両 *Aru ichi mon nai sen ryō.*

To have one *mon* is better than not to have a thousand *ryō*.
[A bird in the hand is worth two in the bush.]

The age-old principle here contrasts present possession with possible future acquisition and finds the future all too iffy. Note: this proverb is not that well known. For another way of balancing money, see 12, *Ichi-mon oshimi no hyaku-zon*: "One coin saved, a hundred losses."

146.

碁に勝って勝負に負ける *Go ni katte shōbu ni makeru.*

Winning at Go, losing the competition.
[It's not whether you win or lose, but how you play the game; or, winning the battle but losing the war.]

This proverb sets up two priorities: an individual victory doesn't bulk as large as the whole contest, and one must keep a proper sense of proportion. See 45, *Makeru ga kachi*: "To lose is to win."

147.

着れば着寒し *Kireba kizamushi.*

The more you wear, the colder you feel.
[The greedy are never satisfied.]

Though this sentence sounds almost nonsensical if taken literally, it's based on a psychological truth: The more you have, the more you want. For a modern parallel, see the poet T. S. Eliot's line from "Gerontion": "the giving famishes the craving."

148.

士族の商法 *Shizoku no shōhō.*

A warrior's business practices.

[A fish out of water.]

People expect a samurai to excel at military matters, not at accounting; by extension, "to each his own trade," which is the essence of 27, *Mochi wa mochi-ya*: "For rice cakes, go to the rice-cake maker." As a historical note: during the Meiji Restoration, retired samurai really did try their hands at business.

149.

燈台下暗し *Tōdai moto kurashi.*

Darkness at the base of the lighthouse.
[Sometimes you can't see the forest for the trees.]

This statement about selective blindness, especially about what's right
in front of one, has many parallels; see, for instance, 99, *Issun wa yami*:
"Darkness lies one inch ahead."

150.

えん豆は日陰でもはじける *Endō wa hikage de mo hajikeru.*

Beans grow even in the shade.

[To everything there is a season.]

This agricultural metaphor emphasizes the eventual maturity of all living things, when one comes into one's own. Similar to this is *Igaguri mo uchi kara wareru* (いが栗も内から割れる): "A chestnut will split from inside itself." When the time comes, one will accomplish one's purpose.

151.

河豚は食いたし命は惜しし

Fugu wa kuitashi inochi wa oshishi.

Blowfish is tasty, but life is precious.

[He who plays with fire gets burnt.]

Circumspection, caution, and prudence are all part of the Japanese way of life, yet the Japanese do court danger by eating the poisonous blowfish or *fugu*, which is to say that many proverbs warn against exactly what people are likely to do.

152.

敗軍の将は兵を語らず *Haigun no shō wa hei o katarazu.*
A defeated army's general should not talk about tactics.
[People in glass houses shouldn't throw stones.]

This saying scolds boasters or those who simply talk too much. Many proverbs warn against what comes out of the mouth, but a Western parallel here is "Actions speak louder than words." Compare to 22, *Tamago to chikai wa kudake-yasui*: "Eggs and vows are easily broken."

隠すことは口より出すな

153.

隠すことは口より出すな　*Kakusu koto wa kuchi yori dasuna.*

Do not let secrets leave your mouth.

[Loose lips sink ships.]

Here is yet another warning against talking too much, in this case betraying privileged knowledge. Gossip is a staple of entertainment—and danger—everywhere. See 19, *Kuchi wa wazawai no moto*: "The mouth is the cause of calamity."

154.

居は気を移す *Kyo wa ki o utsusu.*

One's residence affects one's mood.
[You are what you eat.]

Traditional Japanese dwellings are carefully constructed to harmonize with natural surroundings, with the implication that "you are a part of where you live." The proverb reflects a psychological truth, that where one dwells is significant. Compare to *Uji yori sodachi* (氏より育ち): "Breeding over birth."

155.

昔は今の鏡 *Mukashi wa ima no kagami.*

The past is the mirror of today.

[History goes in cycles.]

The Japanese have a sense of living tradition, which means that the past and present are not separate but fused instead. This sentiment is also expressed in the saying *Furuki o tazunete atarashiki o shiru* (故きを温ねて新しきを知る): "To understand new things, study the old." Contrary to this attitude is *Mukashi wa mukashi, ima wa ima* (昔は昔今は今): "The past is the past, and now is now."

156.

木に餅がなる *Ki ni mochi ga naru.*

Rice cakes grow on trees.

[Money doesn't grow on trees.]

This proverb is one of a series suggesting impossible windfalls (see 70, *Yanagi no shita ni itsu-mo dojō wa inai*: "One cannot always find a fish under a willow"). Rice cakes are often used as emblems of good fortune, as in *Tana kara bota mochi* (棚からぼたもち): "A rice cake falls from the shelf," referring to an all-too-rare lucky break.

157.

失敗は成功の母 *Shippai wa seikō no haha.*

Failure is the mother of success.

[Experience is the best teacher.]

The backbone of many proverbs is the importance of hard experience. Adversity teaches one. See 100, *Nana-korobi, yaoki*: "Fall down seven times, get up eight."

158.

芸は身の仇 *Gei wa mi no ada.*

One's art may be one's enemy.
[Don't get carried away.]

Herein lies a warning against becoming too obsessed. Underlying the proverb is an urge for moderation. Of course, this saying doesn't mean to avoid all *gei* or art; see *Gei wa mi o tasukeru* (芸は身を助ける): "Art helps the body," meaning "A skill helps one get by."

暖簾に腕押し

159.

暖簾に腕押し *Noren ni ude-ōshi.*

Strong-arming a shop curtain.

[Like boxing with a shadow.]

The comical image suggests the silly notion of fighting against what doesn't resist, or starting a useless contest. For another humorous way of putting this struggle, consider *Tōfu ni kasugai* (豆腐にかすがい): "[Applying] a clamp on a bean curd."

160.

家来と成らねば家来は使えぬ

Kerai to naraneba kerai wa tsukaenu.

Unless you have been a servant, you cannot use a servant.

[It takes one to know one.]

The Japanese may be class-conscious, but that implies not so much snobbery as noblesse oblige, the obligations of the ruling class. See *Hito o tsukau wa tsukawaruru* (人を使うは使われる): "To help a person is to be helped."

161.

楽しみに女なし男なし *Tanoshimi ni onna nashi otoko nashi.*

In the pursuit of pleasure, there is no difference between a woman and a man.

[What's sauce for the goose is sauce for the gander.]

The truth behind this proverb is questionable, especially considering the eternal divide between the sexes. But the assertion can also be taken broadly: everyone wants some fun.

162.

鉛は刀となすべからず *Namari wa katana to nasu-bekarazu.*

Lead should not be made into a sword.

[You can't make a silk purse from a sow's ear.]

All the hard work in the world won't make unfit materials into desired objects. This saying concerns the proper use of materials, since lead is too soft a metal for a sharp weapon.

鳥は古巣に帰る

163.

鳥は古巣に帰る　*Tori wa furusu ni kaeru.*

Birds return to old nests.

[There's no place like home.]

This observation turns the proverb "Familiarity breeds contempt" on its head: Familiarity breeds comfort, where one has lived before and has acquired experience. Note the verb *kaeru*, which means not just "to return" but "to go home." See *Kokyo bōji-gatashi* (故郷忘じ難し): "It's hard to forget one's hometown."

164.

心は二つ身は一つ　*Kokoro wa futatsu mi wa hitotsu.*

One body for two hearts.

[To be of two minds.]

This phrase neatly sums up ambivalence, or wishing in two directions. A harsher version of this truth is *Nito o ou-mono wa itto o mo ezu* (二兎を追う者は一兎をも得ず): "The person who chases after two rabbits won't catch even one."

165.

破れ鍋に綴じ蓋 *Ware-nabe ni toji-buta.*

A repaired lid on a broken pot.
[Two of a kind.]

Here is a humble image for a pair of anything, both somewhat damaged, not necessarily alike, but enough so to go together. The saying often refers to a couple, as in the saying *Nita mono fūfu* (似た者夫婦): "A couple who resemble each other."

166.

文はやりたし書く手は持たず
Fumi wa yaritashi kaku-te wa motazu.

I want to write but have no writing hand.
[Pen in hand, heart in mouth.]

The world is full of would-be writers, many of whom can't seem to fill a page. This image often applies to a romantic soul who wants to send a love letter, or an illiterate person who wishes to put something into print.

童べに花持たせるごとし

167.

童べに花持たせるごとし *Waranbe ni hana motaseru gotoshi.*

Like giving flowers to a child.

[Like a bull in a china shop.]

This proverb, not much in use, is one of many that depends on an image of inappropriateness, in this instance rough handling for a delicate object. Compare to 148, *Shizoku no shōhō*: "A warrior's business practices"; and 177, *Setchin de yari o tsukau yō*: "Like wielding a spear in a toilet."

168.

一葉落ちて天下の秋を知る

Ichiyō ochite tenka no aki o shiru.

One leaf falls, and you know that autumn is in the land.

[A robin is a harbinger of spring.]

The Japanese are close watchers of nature and its small patterns within larger ones, as in good haiku. A microcosm represents a macrocosm. Here, one leaf ready to drop stands for all of fall.

169.

息の香臭きは主しらず *Iki no kusaki wa nushi shirazu.*

The possessor of bad breath does not notice the odor.
[Before complaining of the mote in your brother's eye, first remove
the beam from your own.]

To judge one's own qualities is hard because one lacks perspective and
objectivity. Compare to *Jibun no bon no kubo wa miezu* (自分の盆の
窪は見えず): "One can't see the back of one's own neck." The source of
the English version is from the Bible, Matthew 7.3: "And why bcholdest
thou the mote that is in thy brother's eye, but considerest not the beam
that is in thine own eye?"

170.

上知と下愚とは移らず *Jōchi to kagu to wa utsurazu.*

Wise men and fools do not change.
[The pure of heart stay pure.]

This saying comes from the *Analects* of Confucius. Most societies have a special regard for those mentally different from the norm, as if they occupy a higher state. The attitude may also be condescending, however, as in *Kawara wa migaite mo tama ni naranu* (瓦は磨いても玉にならぬ): "Polish a tile, and it still won't become a jewel."

171.

袖から火事 *Sode kara kaji.*

A fire from a kimono sleeve.

[For want of a nail, the kingdom was lost.]

Because most houses in old Japan were wooden, even small fires could turn quite serious, as in the 1657 *Hurisode kaji* (振り袖火事), a devastating blaze from a sleeve set alight during a Buddhist ceremony. Many proverbs teach how the seemingly trivial can lead to great significance, though sometimes with a positive effect, as in the Western saying "Great oaks from little acorns grow."

172.

病を護りて医を忌む *Yamai o mamorite i o imu.*

Shun the doctor to protect one's disease.
[Hide your shame.]

"Don't wash dirty linen in public" is a directive with particular force in a shame-based society, where people tend to conceal scandal. This proverb includes the idea that addressing the problem calls attention to it, thus perhaps worsening it.

173.

痘痕もえくぼ *Abata mo ekubo.*

Even pockmarks may look like dimples.
[Love is blind.]

If love is the triumph of illusion over substance, as a wit once explained, then love has partial eyes. This proverb is yet another of the many sayings about appearance versus reality. Consider also *Hage ga san-nen me ni tsukaenu* (禿が三年眼につかえぬ): "After three years, one doesn't notice the other's baldness."

174.

熱い物は冷めやすい *Atsui mono wa same-yasui.*

Hot things cool easily.
[The hotter the flame, the quicker it dies.]

This proverb is in a sense a corrective to saying 173, showing a more sober view of passion. The variant *Atsui koi wa same-yasui* (熱い恋は冷めやすい) refers specifically to *koi* or love. More generally, the proverb warns against extremes that will lead to letdowns.

175.

瓢箪で鯰を押さえる *Hyōtan de namazu o osaeru.*

To pin down a catfish with a gourd.
Slippery as an eel.

"The right tool for the right job" is an obvious subtext for this proverb
and its absurd mismatch between a smooth, round surface to hold fast
a wet, slippery item. The expression is a metaphor for being clumsy or
awkward or just impractical.

176.

水底の針を捜す *Minasoko no hari o sagasu.*

To search for a needle at the bottom of the water.
[To look for a needle in a haystack.]

Herein is an image of futility, specifically a ridiculously difficult quest, because the item is so hard to spot against its surroundings. Note that the Western version proposes an even tougher task, since needles resemble stalks of hay.

雪隠で槍を使うよう

177.

雪隠で槍を使うよう *Setchin de yari o tsukau yō.*

Like wielding a spear in a toilet.

[No room to swing a cat.]

The lack of space in most Japanese homes may have given rise to this image, though by extension it implies clumsy maneuvering, in general. For another such mismatch, see 148, *Shizoku no shōhō*: "A warrior's business practices." Note: the famed general Takeda Shingen (1521-73) always requested spacious bathrooms wherever he lodged.

縁は異なもの

178.

縁は異なもの *En wa i na mono.*

Marriage is a curious thing.
[Fate has a hand in weddings.]

Human relationships and marriages in particular are the subject of many proverbs. In this saying, a lot depends on the interpretation of the character *i*, which may also be translated as "strange" or even "piquant." A variant of this proverb, *En wa aji na mono* (縁は味なもの), replaces *i* with *aji* or "zesty."

179.
百戦百勝は善の善なる者に非ず
Hyakusen hyakushō wa zen no zen naru mono ni arazu.

A hundred victories in a hundred battles is good, but the virtuous man does otherwise.

[The best defense is avoidance.]

As repositories of common sense and practicality, most proverbs do not advocate violence. Instead, they suggest appeasement or even flight as less damaging. This saying comes from a Chinese manual on military tactics. See 45, *Makeru ga kachi*: "To lose is to win."

180.

裸で物を落とす例なし

Hadaka de mono o otosu tameshi nashi.

There are no instances of a naked person dropping things.
[Nothing left to hide.]

This proverb is a humorous version of the observation that the less one has, the less one has to lose. As a historical note: *sagemono*, small receptacles hanging from belts and sashes, often made up for the lack of pockets in traditional Japanese clothing.

181.

横車を押す *Yokoguruma o osu.*

To push a cart sideways.

[To push a rock up a mountain.]

Many proverbs talk of difficult tasks, such as finding a needle at the bottom of the water (176), but this saying also imagines trying to move something in a direction it ordinarily doesn't go. Compare to 16, *Sendō ōku shite fune yama ni noboru*: "Too many boatmen will bring a boat up a mountain."

好きこそ物の上手なれ

i82.

好きこそ物の上手なれ *Suki-koso mono no jōzu nare.*

One becomes skilled at the very thing one likes.
[Do what you love, and success will follow.]

This proverb almost seems circular, or at least has the logical flow of a good syllogism: If practice makes perfect, and you repeat what you like, you'll become adept at it. Yet the Japanese also have the phrase *heta no yoku-zuki* (下手の横好き), meaning "I'm bad at it, but I like it."

183.

隣の花は赤い　*Tonari no hana wa akai.*

The neighbor's flowers are red.
[The grass is greener on the other side of the fence.]

An age-old psychological insight is contained in this proverb, that people want what they don't have. The Bible calls it coveting and considers it a sin, but this proverb notes how human it is. A counterpoint showing domestic pride is *Tonari no shiro-meshi yori uchi no awameshi* (隣りの白飯より内の粟飯): "Our millet is better than the neighbor's white rice."

184.

粋は身を食う *Sui wa mi o kuu.*

Fashion eats up the body.
[One must suffer to be beautiful.]

Here is the price one pays for chasing after the latest fad, not to be confused with suffering for one's art. Cf. 95: *Kyō no kidaore, Ōsaka no kuidaore*: "Kyoto people ruin themselves for clothing, Osaka people for food."

185.

寺の隣にも鬼が住む　*Tera no tonari ni mo oni ga sumu.*

Devils, too, live alongside the temple.
[Good and evil live side by side.]

Embodied in this maxim is a Manichean view; that is, a world with active good and evil principles—or yin and yang, always with a spot of one quality mixed into its opposite. It also serves as a caution, to be careful in even the most innocent-seeming setting.

186.

自分の頭の蠅を追え *Jibun no atama no hae o oe.*

Brush the flies away from your own head.

[Mind your own business.]

Japanese society has always been stratified, which means to stick to one's ways and not explore other avenues. Compare to 30, *Inu mo arukeba bō ni ataru:* "A dog that walks around will find a stick," in the sense of being punished for curiosity.

187.

棒ほど願って針ほど叶う *Bō hodo negatte hari hodo kanau.*

Ask for as much as a pole and be given only a needle.
[You can't always get what you want.]

This saying is an arch observation on the nature of people's generosity—
or the lack of it, perhaps because people tend to ask for or grab too
much, as in the Western dictum "Give them an inch, and they'll take a
mile," or, as in 188, *Hisashi o kashite omoya o torareru*: "Lend the eaves
and the main building will be taken."

188.

庇を貸して母屋を取られる

Hisashi o kashite omoya o torareru.

Lend the eaves and the main building will be taken.

[Give them an inch and they'll take a mile.]

In a sense the mirror opposite of 187, *Bō hodo negatte hari hodo kanau*: "Ask for as much as a pole and be given only a needle," this proverb has a humorous Western version: "No good deed goes unpunished."

189.

井戸端の茶碗 *Idobata no chawan.*

A teacup on the edge of a well.

[A house of cards.]

A delicate object all too apt to fall and smash is the image here, by extension a precarious situation, one likely to collapse or break up at any moment. Note: this proverbial expression is no longer well recognized.

190.

知らざるは誤れるに勝る

Shirazaru wa ayamareru ni masaru.

Better not to know than to be wrong.

[Better to remain silent and be thought ignorant than to open one's mouth and remove all doubt.]

The role of shame in Japanese society is a powerful deterrent to taking chances. "Don't do that," say Japanese mothers to their children. "People will laugh at you." Note that, though this proverb is not in much vogue, the sentiment behind it is quite common.

191.

裾取って肩へ継ぐ　*Suso totte kata e tsugu.*

Taking from the hem to patch the shoulder.
[Robbing Peter to pay Paul.]

Many proverbs describe hard times and how to cope with poverty. The Western notion about "making both ends meet" pertains, though the solution here is temporary. Note: People nowadays tend to buy new clothes when old ones rip, but an earlier era believed in sewing and darning.

192.

鰯の頭も信心から *Iwashi no kashira mo shinjin kara.*

Put faith even in a sardine head.

[Everyone has to believe in something.]

The absurdity of the image, talking to a dead fish, is balanced by the serious subject of belief. Compare to 2, *Hiza tomo dango*: "Consult anyone, even your knees." Note: on *setsubun*, the day before spring, some traditional Japanese pierce sardine heads on holly branches and hang them from their door to drive away evil spirits

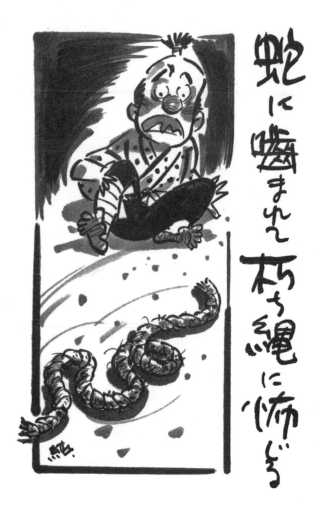

193.

蛇に嚙まれて朽ち縄に怖じる

Hebi ni kamarete kuchi-nawa ni ojiru.

A person bitten by a snake will fear a rotted rope.

[A burnt cat will avoid a cold stove.]

Proverbs teach the value of experience, but this humorous version describes the perils of over-generalizing from an incident. By extension, it warns against hasty judgment. A similar proverb is *Atsumono ni korite namasu o fuku* (羹 に懲りて 膾 を吹く): "Learning from hot soup, blow on cold salad." Compare 193 to the opposite, 142, *Mekura hebi ni ojizu*: "The blind do not fear snakes."

194.

金が金を呼ぶ *Kane ga kane o yobu.*

Money calls to money.

[The rich get richer.]

This observation about capitalism is true of other properties, as well, such as luck or friends: when one has amassed a quantity of something, other items of that type tend to join the mix. A version of this proverb exists in Latin: *Nummus nummum parit:* "Money gives birth to money."

195.

雨垂れ石を穿つ *Amadare ishi o ugatsu.*

Raindrops will wear through a stone.

[Slow and steady wins the race.]

Slow accumulation and attrition are chronicled over and over in Japanese proverbs, as in 32, *Chiri mo tsumoreba yama to naru*: "Even dust amassed will grow into a mountain." Here, the opposite effect is described, but with the same sustained effort.

泥中の蓮

196.

泥中の蓮 *Deichū no hasu.*

A lotus flower in the mire.
[A diamond in the rough.]

The lotus blossom, a salient symbol, represents enlightenment in Buddhism. To place it in the mud is to establish a contrast between an object of high esteem and low surroundings. But perhaps only a careful observer can spot its true worth.

見たいが病

197.

見たいが病 *Mitai ga yamai.*

Wanting to see is a weakness.
[Curiosity killed the cat.]

Japanese society does not much reward inquiring minds; in feudal Japan, it sometimes punished them with death. Western civilization, too, through repressive religion and politics, has a history of discouraging free inquiry. This proverb acknowledges the dangers of investigation.

198.

燈滅せんとして火を増す *Tō messen to shite hi o masu.*

A candle flares up just before extinguishing.
[Old coals burn brightest.]

Life is not just a simple descent after middle age, and individuals near death may exhibit sudden life. As Shakespeare writes in sonnet 73: "In me thou see'st the glowing of such fire / That on the ashes of his youth doth lie."

199.

無くて七癖 *Nakute nana kuse.*

Nothing if not seven habits.

[Everyone has a few peculiarities.]

Despite the Japanese tendency toward conformity, village life tends
to tolerate eccentricities. This proverb also acknowledges that people's
personalities are composites, characterized by more than just one trait.

200.

折れるよりなびけ *Oreru yori nabike.*

Better to bow than to break.
[Be like the willow, not like the oak.]

Adapting to circumstances is crucial to survival; many proverbs record this truth. Compare to 82, *Yanagi ni kaze*: "A willow before the wind"; and 179, *Hyakusen hyakushō wa zen no zen naru mono ni arazu*: "A hundred victories in a hundred battles is good, but the virtuous man does otherwise."

Index of English Language Proverbs and Expressions

Index of Concepts and Keywords by Proverb

evil 13, 102, 117, 185
excess 21, 23, 95, 110
exhaustion 68
experience 67, 157, 160, 193
expression 127
extremes 18, 128, 158, 174, 187
eyes 127
face 33
failure 3, 100, 157, 190
faith 192
falling 100, 122, 168
familiarity 39, 163
fart 52
fashion 184
fate 66
fear 48, 103, 142, 193
field 15
fingernail 49
fire 48, 171, 198
fish 64, 70, 130, 133, 175
flower 20, 31, 104, 167, 183, 196
fly 186
food 31, 95, 129, 132
fool 44, 62, 93, 170
foot 84
force 34
formality 39
forget (see memory)
friendship 39, 51
frog 42
fruit 141
frustration 93, 134
futility 52, 68, 93, 108, 109, 115, 134, 159, 175, 176, 177, 181
general 152
generosity 9, 111, 144, 188
genius 112
gift 9
Go 146
goodness 61, 139, 185
gossip 13
gourd 175
government 29
grass 90
gratitude 9
greed 59, 104, 107, 147, 187, 188
guest 73
guilt 89
habit 199
hairy 26
hammer 43

hand 84, 166
hardship 33, 36, 48, 76, 94, 134
haste 56, 61
hawk 72
head 60, 186
headache 81
hearing 120
heart 55, 79, 107, 138, 164
heaven 120
heedlessness 99, 149, 169
hell 120
hem 191
heredity 42
hiding 60, 72
hole 6
home 154, 163
honesty 127
honor 96
horse 1, 58, 115
hospitality 73
hot 119, 174
humility 152
hunger 91, 96
hurry 56
ignorance 142, 149, 190
imitation 8, 21, 49, 140
impatience(see patience)
impermanence 7, 141, 168
impossibility 15, 29, 81, 93
impracticality (see practicality)
inability (see ability)
inappropriateness (see appropriateness)
incense 89
incompatibility (see compatibility)
indecision 164
individuality 46, 199
industry 32, 36, 143, 195
ingenuity 78, 106
injury 94, 133
injustice 117
innocence 54
inquiry (see curiosity)
insatiability 147
insect 25
insularity 53
intemperance 23, 95
jacket 9
job 27, 90
journey 5, 47, 51
judgment 113
kimono 171
kindness 135, 138

knee 2
Kyoto 50, 95
lacquer 92
laugh 116
lead 162
leaf 168
learning 55, 67, 74, 91, 118, 124, 143
leftover 75
leisure 36
lid 35, 165
life 7, 51, 151
lighthouse 149
lion 102
liquid 119
listening 137
livelihood 27, 90
logic (see reason)
loss 12, 45, 146 (also see defeat)
lotus 196
love 26, 65, 173
luck 69, 70, 75, 156
lumbago 81
man 23, 46, 161
marriage 21, 178
materialism 21, 107
maturity 112, 150
meal 129
medicine 77
meditation 113
memory 47, 67, 119
mire 196
mirror 20, 155
miser 59
mistake (see failure)
moderation 23, 158
mon 145
money 107, 194
monkey 3
mood 154
moon 104, 129
mortar 67
mountain 16, 32, 98
mouth 19, 77, 127, 153
nail 43
naked 180
narrow-mindedness (see insularity)
nature 48, 98
navel 93, 116
needle 115, 176, 187
neighbor 183
nest 163
obeying 14, 71